I0504682

THE GREEN DIGITAL NOMAD

SUSTAINABLE TRAVEL AND WORK PRACTICES

CONNECTNOMADS   contact@connectnomads.com

THE GREEN DIGITAL NOMAD

This book will cover eco-friendly practices in travel, work, and daily life, offering insights into reducing carbon emissions, supporting sustainable businesses, and making responsible choices. We'll discuss strategies for minimizing your environmental impact, from choosing greener transportation to adopting energy-efficient work habits. Along the way, we'll also share resources and advice for connecting with like-minded individuals and fostering a green digital nomad community.

CONNECT NOMADS DIGITAL ELIBRARY

What is ConnectNomads.com

ConnectNomads.com is a comprehensive platform designed for digital nomads and remote workers seeking resources, guidance, and community. Offering valuable information on topics such as remote work opportunities, travel planning, and lifestyle management, ConnectNomads.com aims to empower location-independent professionals to thrive in their careers while exploring the world.

THE GREEN DIGITAL NOMAD: SUSTAINABLE TRAVEL AND WORK PRACTICES

Discover a greener way to live and work as a digital nomad with "The Green Digital Nomad." This essential guide offers practical advice on adopting eco-friendly practices in travel, work, and daily life. Learn how to reduce your carbon emissions, support sustainable businesses, and make responsible choices that minimize your environmental impact. Explore strategies for greener transportation, energy-efficient work habits, and building a supportive green digital nomad community. Packed with resources and insights, this book empowers you to embrace a sustainable lifestyle and become an inspiring advocate for positive change in the world of digital nomadism.

Our Digital Library

The ConnectNomads.com library offers members a diverse collection of free eBooks, providing invaluable insights and practical advice on a variety of topics related to the digital nomad lifestyle. From remote work strategies to travel tips and personal development, these eBooks are a valuable resource for location-independent professionals seeking to enhance their skills, knowledge, and overall experience.

Please visit http://www.connectnomad.com to see if there are any other publications which might interest you.

Mentions

We would like to clarify that throughout this book, we have not received any monetary gain or inducements for mentioning any connections, people, or resources. Our primary goal is to share valuable insights and tips that can genuinely help digital nomads in their journey of self-discovery and personal growth. The only exceptions to this are individuals or resources identified as ConnectNomads Members on our website. These members are part of our community and support our mission. We maintain transparency and prioritize the authenticity of the information shared, ensuring that our readers can trust the guidance provided in this book.

CONTENTS

Contents

THE GREEN DIGITAL NOMAD ....

CONNECT NOMADS DIGITAL ELIBRARY...

CONTENTS...

Introduction...

Understanding Your Environmental Footprint ....

Sustainable Travel Practices..

Green Work Practices ....

Sustainable Daily Living ....

Offsetting Your Carbon Emissions ....

Building a Green Digital Nomad Community..

Conclusion...

Appendices..

INTRODUCTION

The Rise of Digital Nomadism

In recent years, the rise of digital technology and an increasingly connected world have enabled a growing number of professionals to work remotely. This shift has given birth to the digital nomad lifestyle, where individuals can travel and explore the world while earning a living through their online work. This new way of living offers unparalleled freedom and flexibility, allowing people to pursue their passions, experience new cultures, and broaden their horizons.

The digital nomad lifestyle, however, is not without its environmental consequences. Traveling frequently, often by air, can have a significant carbon footprint. Additionally, remote work can lead to increased energy consumption through the use of electronic devices and a reliance on internet connectivity. These factors, combined with the daily choices digital nomads make, can have a lasting impact on our planet.

As the digital nomad community continues to grow, it is essential that we consider the environmental implications of this lifestyle and strive to make more sustainable choices. "The Green Digital Nomad: Sustainable Travel and Work Practices" aims to shed light on the environmental impact of the digital nomad lifestyle and provide practical tips for reducing your footprint while still enjoying the freedom and adventure that comes with being a digital nomad.

By embracing a more sustainable approach to the digital nomad lifestyle, you can continue to explore the world while taking steps to protect our planet for future generations. We hope that this book will inspire and empower you to make a positive difference, both in your own life and in the global community.

The Environmental Impact of a Global Lifestyle

As digital nomads, we often enjoy the benefits of experiencing different cultures and landscapes around the world. However, it is important to recognize that this global lifestyle comes with a substantial environmental impact. In this section, we will explore the various ways in which the digital nomad lifestyle contributes to environmental degradation and discuss the importance of making conscious choices to reduce our ecological footprint.

1. Carbon emissions from travel: One of the most significant environmental impacts of a global lifestyle is the carbon emissions generated from various modes of transportation. Air travel, in particular, is a major contributor to greenhouse gas emissions, with a single long-haul flight producing a substantial amount of CO_2. Overland travel, such as by car or bus, also adds to your carbon footprint, albeit at a lesser extent than air travel.

2. Energy consumption: The digital nomad lifestyle often relies heavily on electronic devices and internet connectivity, both of which require energy. The more gadgets we use and the longer we use them; the more energy we consume. This energy consumption contributes to greenhouse gas emissions, particularly when sourced from non-renewable resources like fossil fuels.

3. Waste generation: Traveling and living in different places often means using disposable items, such as single-use plastics, food packaging, and disposable personal care products. The

waste generated by these items can contribute to pollution, harm wildlife, and strain local waste management systems, especially in developing countries.

4. Resource use: The digital nomad lifestyle can lead to increased demand for natural resources, such as water and energy, in the destinations we visit. This can put pressure on local ecosystems and contribute to resource depletion, particularly in regions already facing scarcity issues.

5. Impact on local communities: A growing number of digital nomads can lead to increased demand for housing, transportation, and other services in popular destinations. This can result in increased costs for local residents, as well as environmental degradation from over-tourism and the development of infrastructure to support the influx of travellers.

By understanding these environmental impacts, digital nomads can take action to mitigate their ecological footprint and make more sustainable choices in their travel, work, and daily life. The following chapters in this book will delve into practical strategies and tips for reducing your impact while still enjoying the freedom and adventure of the digital nomad lifestyle.

UNDERSTANDING YOUR ENVIRONMENTAL FOOTPRINT

The Basics of Carbon Emissions and Travel

To make informed decisions about reducing your environmental impact as a digital nomad, it's essential to understand the relationship between carbon emissions and travel. In this section, we will explore the basics of carbon emissions, how they contribute to climate change, and their connection to various modes of transportation.

1. What are carbon emissions? Carbon emissions refer to the release of carbon dioxide (CO_2) and other greenhouse gases into the atmosphere as a result of human activities, such as burning fossil fuels, deforestation, and industrial processes. These emissions trap heat in the atmosphere, causing global temperatures to rise and leading to climate change.

2. How do travel and transportation contribute to carbon emissions? Transportation is a major source of carbon emissions, accounting for a significant percentage of global greenhouse gas emissions. The burning of fossil fuels, such as gasoline, diesel, and jet fuel, releases CO_2 and other harmful pollutants into the atmosphere. Different modes of transportation have varying levels of emissions, with air travel being the most carbon-intensive form of transport on a per-passenger basis.

3. Comparing different modes of transportation:
   - Air travel: Aircraft release a large amount of CO_2 and other greenhouse gases per passenger, particularly on long-haul flights. The emissions from air travel also have a more significant warming effect than those released at ground level due to the altitude at which they are released.
   - Car travel: Personal vehicles, especially those with low fuel efficiency, can generate substantial emissions. However, carpooling or using electric or hybrid vehicles can help reduce the carbon footprint of car travel.

- Bus and coach travel: Buses and coaches generally have lower carbon emissions per passenger than cars and planes, making them an eco-friendlier option for overland travel.
- Train travel: Trains, particularly electric ones, tend to have lower emissions per passenger compared to cars and planes, making them a more sustainable choice for long-distance travel.
- Cycling and walking: These non-motorized forms of transportation produce no direct carbon emissions and have numerous health benefits as well.

Understanding the carbon emissions associated with various modes of transportation can help digital nomads make more informed decisions about their travel choices. By opting for less carbon-intensive forms of transport whenever possible, digital nomads can significantly reduce their environmental footprint and contribute to the fight against climate change.

Calculating Your Carbon Footprint

As a digital nomad, being aware of your carbon footprint can help you make more eco-conscious decisions about your travel, work, and daily life. Calculating your carbon footprint involves estimating the total amount of greenhouse gas emissions caused by your actions and lifestyle choices. Here's a step-by-step guide to help you calculate your carbon footprint:

1. List your major sources of emissions: To get started, identify the primary sources of carbon emissions in your life. For digital nomads, these sources typically include:
   - Transportation (flights, car travel, public transport, etc.)
   - Accommodations (energy consumption for heating, cooling, lighting, etc.)
   - Work-related energy use (electronic devices, internet usage, etc.)
   - Daily living (diet, shopping habits, waste generation, etc.)

2. Collect data: Gather information on your activities and choices related to each emission source. This data might include:
   - The number and distance of flights taken in a year
   - Fuel consumption or mileage of car travel
   - Type of public transport used, and distance travelled
   - Energy consumption of accommodations (electricity, heating, etc.)
   - Types and usage of electronic devices
   - Dietary habits (meat consumption, food miles, etc.)
   - Waste generation and recycling habits

3. Use a carbon footprint calculator: There are several online tools available that can help you calculate your carbon footprint based on the data you've collected. Some of these calculators include:
   - The Nature Conservancy's Carbon Footprint Calculator (global): https://www.nature.org/en-us/get-involved/how-to-help/carbon-footprint-calculator/
   - The Carbon Footprint Calculator (UK): https://www.carbonfootprint.com/calculator.aspx
   - The EPA's Carbon Footprint Calculator (US): https://www3.epa.gov/carbon-footprint-calculator/

These calculators will ask you to input information about your activities and choices, and they will estimate your carbon footprint in terms of CO2 equivalent (CO2e) emissions. Keep in mind that the accuracy of these calculations depends on the quality and comprehensiveness of the data you provide.

4. Analyse your results: Once you've calculated your carbon footprint, take a closer look at the results to identify areas where you can make improvements. Focus on the emission sources with the highest impact and consider how you can reduce your footprint through changes in your travel, work, and daily life.

5. Set goals and track progress: Set realistic goals for reducing your carbon footprint and track your progress over time. This can help you stay motivated and committed to making more sustainable choices.

6. By calculating your carbon footprint and understanding your impact on the environment, you can take meaningful steps towards reducing your emissions and adopting a more sustainable lifestyle as a digital nomad.

The Impact of Remote Work

Remote work has become an essential aspect of the digital nomad lifestyle, allowing individuals to maintain their careers while traveling the world. While remote work offers numerous benefits, such as flexibility and reduced commuting, it also has some environmental consequences. In this section, we'll discuss the impact of remote work on the environment and explore ways to mitigate these effects.

1. Energy consumption: Working remotely often involves using electronic devices such as laptops, smartphones, and tablets, which consume energy. Additionally, remote work typically relies on internet connectivity, which also has an energy cost. Data centers that power the internet and cloud services consume significant amounts of electricity, contributing to carbon emissions, especially when the energy is sourced from fossil fuels.

2. Electronic waste: The use of electronic devices for remote work can contribute to the generation of electronic waste (e-waste) when devices become obsolete or damaged. E-waste contains hazardous materials that can harm the environment and human health if not properly managed.

3. Resource use: Remote work can increase the demand for resources like electricity and water, particularly in co-working spaces or accommodations with multiple remote workers. This can put pressure on local resources and contribute to resource depletion in some regions.

4. Positive impacts: Despite these environmental concerns, remote work can also have positive environmental impacts. For example, remote work reduces the need for commuting, which can lead to decreased carbon emissions from transportation. Additionally, remote work may result in less demand for office space, potentially reducing the environmental impact of construction and maintenance of office buildings.

To mitigate the environmental impact of remote work, digital nomads can adopt the following strategies:

1. Use energy-efficient devices: Choose energy-efficient laptops, smartphones, and other gadgets that consume less power. Look for devices with Energy Star ratings or other eco-labels indicating energy efficiency.

2. Practice digital minimalism: Limit the number of electronic devices you use and extend their lifespan by maintaining them properly. Dispose of e-waste responsibly by recycling or donating old devices to certified e-waste management programs.

3. Optimize energy consumption: Turn off devices when not in use, enable energy-saving settings, and unplug chargers when they are not in use. Use natural lighting whenever possible and minimize the use of air conditioning or heating.

4. Choose green co-working spaces: Select co-working spaces that prioritize sustainability, such as those with energy-efficient lighting, solar power systems, and eco-friendly materials.

5. Support green energy: If possible, choose accommodations or co-working spaces powered by renewable energy sources, such as solar or wind power.

By being mindful of the environmental impact of remote work and taking steps to reduce this impact, digital nomads can contribute to a more sustainable future while still enjoying the benefits of a location-independent lifestyle.

SUSTAINABLE TRAVEL PRACTICES

Choosing Eco-Friendly Transportation

As a digital nomad, one of the most significant ways to reduce your environmental impact is by opting for eco-friendly transportation. By choosing more sustainable modes of transport, you can help lower your carbon footprint and contribute to the fight against climate change. Here are some tips for selecting eco-friendly transportation options:

1. Prioritize public transportation: Whenever possible, use public transportation, such as buses, trams, subways, or trains, instead of relying on private vehicles. Public transportation is generally more energy-efficient and produces fewer emissions per passenger than personal cars.

2. Choose fuel-efficient vehicles: If using a private vehicle is necessary, opt for a fuel-efficient, hybrid, or electric car to minimize your carbon emissions. Also, consider carpooling or using ride-sharing services to reduce the number of cars on the road.

3. Opt for non-motorized transportation: For shorter distances, consider walking or cycling as these non-motorized forms of transportation produce no direct carbon emissions and offer numerous health benefits.

4. Select eco-friendly air travel: While air travel is the most carbon-intensive form of transportation, there are ways to make it eco-friendlier. Choose direct flights to reduce the emissions generated during take-offs and landings and consider flying with airlines that have a commitment to sustainability, such as those using biofuels or implementing carbon offset programs.

5. Use high-speed trains for long distances: When available, opt for high-speed trains instead of planes for long-distance travel, as they tend to have lower carbon emissions per passenger. Electric trains are particularly eco-friendly, as they produce no direct emissions during operation.

6. Practice slow travel: Embrace the concept of slow travel by staying in one destination for longer periods, reducing the frequency of your transportation needs. This can help you minimize your overall carbon emissions and allow you to gain a deeper appreciation for the places you visit.

7. Offset your carbon emissions: Consider offsetting the carbon emissions associated with your transportation choices by investing in carbon offset projects. These projects help to reduce or remove greenhouse gas emissions elsewhere, balancing out the emissions you generate during your travels.

By consciously choosing eco-friendly transportation options, digital nomads can significantly reduce their environmental impact while still exploring the world and enjoying the freedom that comes with a location-independent lifestyle.

Slow Travel: Reducing Your Footprint Through Longer Stays

Slow travel is an approach to exploring the world that prioritizes a deeper, more immersive experience in each destination rather than rushing from one place to another. By spending more time in one location, digital nomads can reduce their environmental footprint, form meaningful connections with local communities, and gain a richer understanding of the cultures they encounter. Here are some of the benefits of slow travel and tips for incorporating it into your digital nomad lifestyle:

BENEFITS OF SLOW TRAVEL:

1. Reduced transportation emissions: Longer stays in a single destination mean less frequent travel, which results in lower carbon emissions from transportation. This is particularly significant for air travel, which has a high carbon footprint.

2. Lower resource consumption: Staying in one place for an extended period allows you to establish a more sustainable routine, including shopping at local markets, cooking your own meals, and minimizing waste generation.

3. Supporting local economies: Slow travel often involves patronizing local businesses, such as accommodations, restaurants, and shops, which can help support the local economy and promote sustainable development.

4. Cultural immersion: By spending more time in one place, you can develop a deeper understanding of the local culture, traditions, and customs. This can lead to more authentic and meaningful experiences during your travels.

5. Reduced travel stress: Slow travel allows for a more relaxed pace, reducing the stress and fatigue associated with frequent, fast-paced travel.

TIPS FOR EMBRACING SLOW TRAVEL:

1. Plan longer stays: When organizing your travel itinerary, schedule longer stays in each destination, ranging from a few weeks to several months.

2. Choose accommodations wisely: Opt for eco-friendly accommodations, such as locally-owned guesthouses or hotels that prioritize sustainability or consider house-sitting or home exchange opportunities.

3. Explore local transportation: Make use of public transportation, bicycles, or walking to explore your destination, reducing your reliance on private vehicles and taxis.

4. Connect with local communities: Engage with local residents by participating in community events, language exchanges, or volunteer opportunities, fostering meaningful connections and cultural exchange.

5. Adopt sustainable habits: Establish eco-friendly routines during your extended stay, such as shopping at local markets, reducing waste, and conserving energy and water.

By embracing slow travel, digital nomads can significantly reduce their environmental footprint while enjoying a more immersive, meaningful, and sustainable travel experience. This approach allows you to maintain the freedom and flexibility of the digital nomad lifestyle while making a positive impact on the planet and the communities you visit.

Supporting Green Accommodations and Local Communities

As a digital nomad, choosing eco-friendly accommodations and supporting local communities can have a significant impact on the environment and the places you visit. Here are some tips to help you make greener choices and contribute positively to the communities you encounter during your travels:

1. Research eco-friendly accommodations: Before booking a place to stay, research accommodations that prioritize sustainability. Look for hotels, guesthouses, or hostels that have eco-friendly practices in place, such as energy-efficient lighting, solar power systems, water-saving measures, and recycling programs. You can also search for eco-labels like Green Globe, LEED, or Green Key certifications to ensure the accommodation meets specific environmental standards.

2. Consider alternative accommodations: Explore alternative lodging options like home exchanges, house-sitting, or locally-owned vacation rentals. These options can be eco-friendlier, as they often have a lower environmental impact than traditional hotels and can provide a more authentic local experience.

3. Support local businesses: When choosing where to eat, shop, or book tours, prioritize locally-owned businesses. By doing so, you help support the local economy, encourage sustainable practices, and promote cultural exchange. Additionally, local businesses often have a smaller environmental footprint compared to large corporations or international chains.

4. Engage in responsible tourism: Be a responsible tourist by respecting local customs, traditions, and the environment. Follow leave-no-trace principles, avoid contributing to over tourism, and respect local flora and fauna. Participate in ecotourism activities that emphasize conservation, responsible behaviour, and the well-being of the local community.

5. Volunteer or support local projects: If possible, seek out opportunities to volunteer or contribute to local initiatives focused on social, environmental, or cultural projects. This can help you form meaningful connections with local communities, support sustainable development, and create a positive impact during your travels.

6. Educate yourself about local issues: Take the time to learn about the social, environmental, and cultural issues affecting the destinations you visit. This understanding can help inform your decisions and actions while traveling, ensuring that you contribute positively to the communities you encounter.

7. Spread awareness: Share your knowledge and experiences with fellow digital nomads and travellers. Encourage others to adopt sustainable practices, support local communities, and make eco-friendly choices during their travels.

By supporting green accommodations and local communities, you can make a tangible difference in the places you visit as a digital nomad. Your choices can help promote sustainability, protect the environment, and contribute to the well-being of the communities that welcome you during your travels.

GREEN WORK PRACTICES

Energy-Efficient Gadgets for Remote Work

As a digital nomad, adopting energy-efficient gadgets and technology for remote work can significantly reduce your environmental impact. Choosing energy-saving devices not only helps you lower your carbon footprint but also contributes to a more sustainable lifestyle. Here are some energy-efficient gadgets and practices to consider for your remote work setup:

1. Energy-efficient laptops: Select a laptop with a high Energy Star rating or another eco-label, indicating that the device meets specific energy efficiency standards. Energy-efficient laptops often have longer battery life and consume less power during operation, reducing your overall energy consumption.

2. LED monitors: If you require an external monitor, choose one with LED technology, which consumes less energy and emits less heat compared to traditional LCD monitors. Look for monitors with an Energy Star rating or other energy-saving certifications.

3. Solar chargers: Invest in a solar-powered charger for your electronic devices, such as smartphones, tablets, or laptops. This allows you to harness renewable energy from the sun, reducing your reliance on grid electricity and lowering your carbon emissions.

4. Smart power strips: Consider using smart power strips, which can automatically shut off power to devices that are not in use or in standby mode. This can help reduce energy waste and lower your electricity consumption.

5. Energy-saving peripherals: Choose energy-efficient peripherals, such as wireless keyboards, mice, and speakers that have low power consumption or built-in power-saving features.

6. Enable power-saving settings: Ensure that you have enabled power-saving settings on your devices, such as sleep or hibernation modes, which can reduce energy consumption when the devices are not in use.

7. Unplug chargers and devices: Remember to unplug chargers and other devices when they are not in use, as they can still draw power even when not actively charging or in standby mode.

8. Keep devices well-maintained: Maintain your electronic devices by keeping them clean, updating software, and replacing worn-out components when needed. Well-maintained devices tend to operate more efficiently, reducing energy consumption and prolonging their lifespan.

By incorporating energy-efficient gadgets and practices into your remote work setup, you can contribute to a greener and more sustainable digital nomad lifestyle. These eco-friendly choices not only help reduce your environmental impact but can also save you money on electricity costs in the long run.

Digital Minimalism: Reducing Your Electronic Waste

Digital minimalism is an approach to technology use that emphasizes intentionality, mindfulness, and simplicity. By adopting digital minimalism, digital nomads can reduce their electronic waste (e-waste) and minimize the environmental impact associated with the production, use, and disposal of electronic devices. Here are some tips for embracing digital minimalism and reducing your electronic waste:

1. Limit your devices: Evaluate your needs and determine which electronic devices are truly essential for your work and personal life. Try to minimize the number of devices you own and use, focusing on multifunctional gadgets that can serve multiple purposes.

2. Choose durable and repairable devices: When purchasing electronic devices, opt for those with a reputation for durability and reparability. Devices that can be easily repaired or upgraded can have a longer lifespan, reducing the frequency with which you need to replace them.

3. Maintain your devices: Take care of your electronic devices by keeping them clean, protecting them from damage, and performing regular software updates. Well-maintained devices tend to have a longer lifespan, reducing the need for frequent replacements and lowering e-waste generation.

4. Repurpose or donate old devices: Instead of discarding old devices, consider repurposing them for a different use, such as turning an old smartphone into a dedicated music player or using an old tablet as a digital photo frame. Alternatively, donate your old devices to charities, schools, or organizations that can refurbish and redistribute them to those in need.

5. Recycle e-waste responsibly: When your electronic devices reach the end of their useful life, recycle them properly by taking them to certified e-waste recycling centers or participating in manufacturer take-back programs. Responsible recycling ensures that hazardous materials are managed safely and that valuable components can be recovered and reused.

6. Reduce digital clutter: Practice digital minimalism by decluttering your digital life, including reducing the number of apps, files, and subscriptions you maintain. This can help extend the lifespan of your devices by freeing up storage space and reducing the need for constant upgrades.

7. Support sustainable technology companies: When purchasing electronic devices, choose products from companies that prioritize sustainability, such as those with strong environmental policies, eco-friendly manufacturing processes, and fair labour practices.

By embracing digital minimalism and reducing your electronic waste, you can contribute to a more sustainable digital nomad lifestyle while minimizing your environmental impact. Adopting these practices can help you simplify your life, save money, and promote the responsible use of technology.

Participating in Local Environmental Initiatives

As a digital nomad, you have the unique opportunity to engage with various communities around the world. By participating in local environmental initiatives, you can actively contribute to the conservation and protection of the environment while forming meaningful connections with local residents. Here are some ideas for getting involved in local environmental initiatives during your travels:

1. Join local clean-up events: Participate in community-organized clean-up events, such as beach, park, or river clean-ups. These events help to remove litter and pollution from natural areas, contributing to a cleaner and healthier environment.

2. Support reforestation projects: Get involved in local tree-planting or reforestation efforts to help combat deforestation, restore habitats, and offset carbon emissions. Many organizations and communities organize tree-planting events that welcome volunteers.

3. Engage in wildlife conservation: Seek out opportunities to volunteer with local wildlife conservation organizations, which may involve tasks such as monitoring wildlife populations, habitat restoration, or community education about local species and ecosystems.

4. Promote environmental education: Offer to give talks or workshops on sustainability, waste reduction, or other environmental topics at local schools, community centers, or events. Sharing your knowledge and passion for the environment can help raise awareness and inspire others to take action.

5. Participate in eco-friendly events: Attend local environmental events, such as Earth Day celebrations, World Environment Day activities, or community sustainability workshops. These events can provide valuable learning opportunities and a chance to network with like-minded individuals and organizations.

6. Partner with local organizations: Collaborate with local environmental organizations, NGOs, or government agencies on projects related to sustainability, conservation, or community development. These partnerships can lead to impactful and long-lasting results for the environment and the community.

7. Advocate for sustainable policies: Support local efforts to advocate for sustainable policies and practices within the community, such as the implementation of recycling programs, the promotion of renewable energy, or the creation of protected natural areas.

By participating in local environmental initiatives, you can actively contribute to the well-being of the places you visit while fostering connections with local residents and organizations. Engaging in these activities allows you to make a tangible difference in the communities you encounter, leaving a positive and lasting impact during your digital nomad journey.

SUSTAINABLE DAILY LIVING

Eco-Friendly Eating and Drinking Habits

As a digital nomad, embracing eco-friendly eating and drinking habits can significantly contribute to a more sustainable lifestyle. By making mindful choices about what and how you consume food and beverages, you can reduce your environmental footprint and support the health of the planet. Here are some tips for adopting eco-friendly eating and drinking habits:

1. Choose local and seasonal produce: Whenever possible, opt for locally-grown and seasonal fruits and vegetables, which have a smaller carbon footprint compared to imported produce. Shopping at local farmers' markets or grocery stores that source from nearby farms can help support the local economy and promote sustainable agriculture.

2. Reduce meat and dairy consumption: Consider adopting a more plant-based diet by reducing your consumption of meat and dairy products, which have a higher environmental impact compared to plant-based foods. You don't need to become a full-time vegetarian or vegan, but incorporating more plant-based meals into your diet can make a significant difference.

3. Minimize food waste: Be mindful of the amount of food you purchase, prepare, and consume to minimize food waste. Plan your meals, store leftovers properly, and use up ingredients before they spoil. Composting food scraps is another excellent way to reduce waste and return nutrients to the soil.

4. Carry reusable items: Bring reusable items such as water bottles, coffee cups, cutlery, and food containers to reduce your reliance on single-use plastics and disposable items. Carrying these items with you can help minimize waste and encourage a more eco-conscious mindset.

5. Support eco-friendly restaurants and cafes: When dining out, choose restaurants and cafes that prioritize sustainability, such as those that source ingredients locally, use eco-friendly packaging, or implement waste-reduction practices. Supporting these businesses can encourage more environmentally responsible practices in the food industry.

6. Cook your own meals: When possible, prepare your own meals using eco-friendly ingredients and techniques. Cooking at home allows you to control the ingredients and packaging and can often result in less waste and a smaller environmental impact compared to dining out.

7. Consume sustainable beverages: Opt for eco-friendly beverages, such as fair-trade coffee or tea, locally-produced wine, or beer, or tap water when available. Avoid bottled water and single-use beverage containers, which contribute to plastic waste and have a higher environmental impact.

By adopting eco-friendly eating and drinking habits, you can contribute to a more sustainable daily life as a digital nomad. These practices not only help reduce your environmental impact but can also lead to healthier, more mindful consumption habits that benefit both you and the planet.

Minimizing Single-Use Plastics

Reducing the use of single-use plastics is crucial for protecting the environment and minimizing plastic pollution in our oceans, rivers, and natural habitats. As a digital nomad, you can play an essential role in minimizing single-use plastics by adopting eco-friendly habits and making conscious choices. Here are some tips for reducing your reliance on single-use plastics:

1. Carry a reusable water bottle: Instead of purchasing bottled water, carry a reusable water bottle with you and refill it from safe water sources. This not only helps reduce plastic waste but can also save you money in the long run.

2. Use reusable shopping bags: Bring your own reusable shopping bags when you go grocery shopping or make other purchases. This can help reduce the number of plastic bags that end up in landfills or the environment.

3. Opt for reusable food containers and cutlery: Invest in a set of reusable food containers, cutlery, and straws to use instead of disposable alternatives when eating out or taking food to go. Many restaurants and cafes are happy to accommodate this request, and some even offer incentives for customers who bring their own containers.

4. Choose products with minimal packaging: When shopping for groceries, toiletries, or other products, opt for items with minimal or eco-friendly packaging. Select products in bulk, choose glass or metal containers over plastic, or look for items with recycled or biodegradable packaging.

5. Refuse single-use items: Politely decline single-use items such as plastic cutlery, straws, or disposable cups when they are offered to you. Make it a habit to carry reusable alternatives and request not to be given single-use plastics.

6. Support businesses that prioritize sustainability: Choose to shop at or support businesses that make efforts to reduce single-use plastics, such as those that use eco-friendly packaging, implement plastic-free policies, or participate in plastic reduction initiatives.

7. Spread awareness: Educate others about the impact of single-use plastics on the environment and share your eco-friendly habits with friends, family, and fellow travellers. Encourage them to join you in reducing their plastic consumption and making more sustainable choices.

By minimizing your use of single-use plastics, you can contribute to a more sustainable lifestyle and help combat plastic pollution. Adopting these eco-friendly habits can lead to a more environmentally conscious mindset, inspiring others to join you in making a positive impact on the planet.

Green Cleaning and Personal Care Products

Using green cleaning and personal care products is an important aspect of sustainable living. These eco-friendly alternatives can help reduce your environmental impact and protect your health from harmful chemicals commonly found in conventional products. Here are some tips for choosing and using green cleaning and personal care products:

1. Look for eco-labels and certifications: When purchasing cleaning and personal care products, look for eco-labels and certifications, such as Green Seal, EcoLogo, or USDA Organic. These labels indicate that the product meets specific environmental and health standards, ensuring they are safer for both you and the environment.

2. Choose biodegradable products: Opt for biodegradable cleaning and personal care products, which break down naturally in the environment and do not contribute to long-lasting pollution. This is particularly important for items like soaps and shampoos, which often end up in waterways after use.

3. Avoid harsh chemicals: Select products that are free of harmful chemicals, such as phosphates, chlorine, parabens, sulphates, and synthetic fragrances. These chemicals can be harmful to both human health and the environment.

4. Use concentrated or refillable products: Choose concentrated cleaning products, which require less packaging and transportation, or opt for refillable products that allow you to reuse containers multiple times. This can help reduce packaging waste and lower your overall environmental footprint.

5. Make your own cleaning products: Consider making your own cleaning products using natural ingredients like vinegar, baking soda, and lemon juice. Homemade cleaning solutions can be just as effective as commercial products and are often more cost-effective and eco-friendly.

6. Use reusable or sustainable personal care items: Opt for reusable or sustainable personal care items, such as bamboo toothbrushes, reusable cotton rounds, or menstrual cups, to reduce waste and plastic consumption associated with disposable products.

7. Conserve water: Be mindful of water usage when using cleaning and personal care products. Turn off the tap when brushing your teeth, take shorter showers, and use eco-friendly settings on appliances like dishwashers and washing machines.

By incorporating green cleaning and personal care products into your daily routine, you can significantly reduce your environmental impact and contribute to a more sustainable lifestyle. These eco-friendly choices not only benefit the environment but can also support your health and well-being by minimizing exposure to harmful chemicals.

OFFSETTING YOUR CARBON EMISSIONS

Carbon Offsetting Programs and How They Work

Carbon offsetting is a method used to counterbalance the greenhouse gas emissions generated by various activities, such as travel, energy consumption, or daily living. Carbon offsetting programs work by investing in projects that reduce, remove, or prevent greenhouse gas emissions, helping to mitigate the impact of your carbon footprint. Here's an overview of how carbon offsetting programs work:

1. Calculation of your carbon footprint: The first step in carbon offsetting is to determine your carbon footprint. This involves estimating the amount of greenhouse gas emissions generated by your activities, such as flights, car travel, energy use, or consumption habits. Many online calculators are available to help you assess your carbon footprint.

2. Selection of offset projects: Carbon offset programs invest in various projects that help reduce, remove, or prevent greenhouse gas emissions. These projects can include renewable energy development (e.g., wind or solar farms), energy efficiency improvements, reforestation or afforestation efforts, methane capture from landfills, and community-based initiatives that promote sustainable practices.

3. Verification and certification: To ensure the credibility and effectiveness of carbon offset projects, independent third-party organizations verify and certify these projects based on established standards and methodologies. Some well-known certification standards include the Verified Carbon Standard (VCS), Gold Standard, and the Climate Action Reserve (CAR).

4. Purchase of carbon credits: Once you've calculated your carbon footprint and selected a certified offset project, you can purchase carbon credits corresponding to the amount of greenhouse gas emissions you wish to offset. The funds from these carbon credit purchases are then used to support the selected project.

5. Monitoring and reporting: Carbon offset projects are regularly monitored to ensure they continue to meet certification standards and effectively reduce or remove greenhouse gas emissions. Project developers are required to provide progress reports and updates on the ongoing success and impact of their projects.

By participating in carbon offsetting programs, you can take responsibility for your environmental impact and support projects that contribute to a more sustainable future. While carbon offsetting should not replace efforts to reduce your emissions directly, it can serve as a valuable tool for addressing the unavoidable emissions associated with your digital nomad lifestyle.

Choosing the Right Offset Project for You

Selecting the right carbon offset project is essential to ensure that your investment has a meaningful impact on mitigating climate change. When choosing an offset project, consider the following factors to make a well-informed decision:

1. Type of project: Carbon offset projects come in various forms, including renewable energy, energy efficiency, reforestation, and methane capture. Consider which type of project aligns best with your values and interests. Some projects may have additional benefits, such as supporting local communities or protecting biodiversity, which you might find appealing.

2. Location: Offset projects can be located in different regions and countries around the world. You may prefer to support a project in a specific region or country that you feel connected to or have visited during your travels as a digital nomad.

3. Certification and standards: Ensure that the offset project you choose is certified by a reputable third-party organization, such as the Verified Carbon Standard (VCS), Gold Standard, or the Climate Action Reserve (CAR). These certifications guarantee that the project meets specific criteria for reducing, removing, or preventing greenhouse gas emissions and is regularly monitored for compliance.

4. Transparency and reporting: Look for projects that provide clear information about their objectives, methodologies, and progress. Transparency in monitoring and reporting helps ensure that the project is effectively delivering on its promised emissions reductions.

5. Co-benefits: Some offset projects may offer additional social, economic, or environmental benefits beyond their primary focus on reducing greenhouse gas emissions. These co-benefits could include job creation, support for local communities, improvement of air and water quality, or protection of endangered species and habitats. Select a project that aligns with your values and priorities in these areas.

6. Reputation and track record: Research the organizations behind the offset project to assess their reputation, track record, and overall credibility. Look for reviews, testimonials, or news articles about the organization and its projects to ensure they have a history of delivering successful and impactful results.

7. Budget: Consider the cost of the carbon credits associated with the offset project. While price should not be the only deciding factor, it is important to find a project that fits within your budget and allows you to offset the desired amount of emissions.

By carefully considering these factors, you can choose a carbon offset project that aligns with your values, interests, and budget. Selecting the right project will help ensure that your investment in carbon offsetting has a meaningful impact on combating climate change and contributes to a more sustainable future.

The Future of Carbon Offsetting

As climate change continues to be a pressing global issue, the role and importance of carbon offsetting are likely to evolve and expand in the coming years. Here are some trends and developments that may shape the future of carbon offsetting:

1. Growing demand for offsets: As more individuals, businesses, and governments become aware of the need to reduce their carbon footprints, the demand for carbon offsets is expected to increase. This growing demand will likely drive the development of new and innovative offset projects and encourage broader participation in offsetting initiatives.

2. Enhanced transparency and accountability: With the increasing importance of carbon offsetting, there is likely to be a greater emphasis on transparency, accountability, and the effectiveness of offset projects. This may lead to the development of more rigorous standards and certification processes, as well as increased scrutiny and reporting requirements for project developers.

3. Technological advancements: New technologies and innovations may play a crucial role in the future of carbon offsetting. Advancements in areas such as carbon capture and storage, direct air capture, and bioenergy with carbon capture and storage (BECCS) could offer new

opportunities for offsetting emissions and contribute to the development of more effective and scalable solutions.

4. Nature-based solutions: There is likely to be a growing focus on nature-based solutions for carbon offsetting, such as reforestation, afforestation, and improved land management practices. These solutions not only sequester carbon but also provide additional benefits, such as preserving biodiversity, improving water quality, and supporting local communities.

5. Integration with climate policies: Carbon offsetting may become more closely integrated with national and international climate policies, such as the Paris Agreement and other emissions reduction commitments. This could lead to the development of new market mechanisms, incentives, and regulations that support and encourage carbon offsetting as a key component of climate action strategies.

6. Increased collaboration: The future of carbon offsetting may involve greater collaboration between governments, businesses, non-governmental organizations (NGOs), and individuals. This collaboration could help to drive the development of more ambitious and effective offsetting initiatives, as well as promote the sharing of knowledge, resources, and best practices.

In conclusion, the future of carbon offsetting is likely to be shaped by a range of factors, including growing demand, enhanced transparency, technological advancements, and increased collaboration.

As the importance of addressing climate change continues to grow, carbon offsetting will likely play an increasingly crucial role in helping individuals, businesses, and governments to mitigate their environmental impact and contribute to a more sustainable future.

BUILDING A GREEN DIGITAL NOMAD COMMUNITY

Networking with Other Eco-Conscious Nomads

Creating a network of like-minded, eco-conscious digital nomads can provide valuable support, resources, and inspiration for your sustainable journey. Connecting with others who share your commitment to environmental responsibility can help you exchange ideas, learn from each other's experiences, and collaborate on projects or initiatives. Here are some tips for networking with other green digital nomads:

1. Join online communities and forums: There are numerous online communities, forums, and social media groups dedicated to sustainable living and eco-conscious travel. Join these groups to connect with other digital nomads, participate in discussions, and share your experiences and knowledge.

2. Attend events and meetups: Keep an eye out for events, conferences, workshops, or meetups focused on sustainability, eco-friendly travel, or remote work. These gatherings can be great opportunities to network with other green digital nomads, learn from experts, and build lasting connections.

3. Engage in co-working spaces: Many co-working spaces attract eco-conscious digital nomads who value sustainability. By working in these spaces, you can meet like-minded individuals, exchange ideas, and collaborate on projects that align with your environmental values.

4. Participate in local environmental initiatives: Joining local environmental initiatives, such as clean-up events, tree planting activities, or conservation projects, can help you connect with other environmentally conscious individuals, including digital nomads. These events also allow you to contribute positively to the local community and environment.

5. Share your journey: Document your green digital nomad journey through blogs, social media, podcasts, or other platforms. Sharing your experiences, tips, and insights can help inspire others and attract like-minded individuals to connect with you.

6. Create or join a green digital nomad network: If you can't find an existing network that suits your needs, consider creating your own green digital nomad group or organization. This can provide a platform for eco-conscious digital nomads to connect, collaborate, and support each other in their sustainable journeys.

7. Engage in skill-sharing and collaboration: Offer your skills and expertise to other green digital nomads or seek out opportunities to learn from others. This exchange of knowledge and resources can help you grow as an eco-conscious individual and foster strong connections within the green digital nomad community.

By building a network of eco-conscious digital nomads, you can strengthen your commitment to sustainability, learn from others, and create lasting connections with like-minded individuals. This supportive community can help you stay motivated, inspired, and accountable in your journey towards a greener, more responsible digital nomad lifestyle.

Sharing Your Journey: Inspiring Others to Go Green

Documenting and sharing your green digital nomad journey can have a powerful impact on inspiring others to adopt more sustainable practices. By showcasing your experiences, challenges, and successes, you can demonstrate the feasibility of an eco-friendly lifestyle and motivate others to make more environmentally responsible choices. Here are some tips for sharing your journey and inspiring others to go green:

1. Blogging: Create a blog to share your experiences, tips, and insights on sustainable travel, remote work, and daily living. Regularly update your blog with informative and engaging content that showcases your commitment to eco-friendly practices and highlights the benefits of a green digital nomad lifestyle.

2. Social media: Use social media platforms, such as Instagram, Facebook, Twitter, or LinkedIn, to document your journey and connect with a broader audience. Share photos, videos, and stories that highlight your sustainable choices, experiences, and the beautiful places you visit. Use relevant hashtags and engage with other green digital nomads to expand your network and reach.

3. Podcasts or video channels: Consider starting a podcast or YouTube channel to discuss your experiences, interview other eco-conscious digital nomads, or share tips on sustainable living. This medium allows you to connect with your audience on a more personal level and can be an effective way to inspire others to adopt green practices.

4. Guest posting and collaborations: Contribute articles or guest posts to established blogs, websites, or magazines focused on sustainability, travel, or remote work. Collaborating with

other content creators can help you reach new audiences and share your message more widely.

5. Public speaking and workshops: Offer to give talks or lead workshops on sustainable living, eco-friendly travel, or green work practices at events, conferences, or meetups. Public speaking engagements can be an effective way to inspire others and share your knowledge and experiences.

6. Networking and community building: Engage with other green digital nomads, participate in online communities, and attend events to build connections and share your journey. Networking can help you inspire others through personal interactions and word-of-mouth recommendations.

7. Lead by example: Perhaps the most powerful way to inspire others is to lead by example. Demonstrate your commitment to sustainability through your actions, choices, and lifestyle. As others see the positive impact of your choices, they may be more likely to consider adopting similar practices.

By sharing your green digital nomad journey and inspiring others to go green, you can contribute to a larger movement towards sustainability and environmental responsibility. Your experiences, challenges, and successes can serve as valuable examples for others, motivating them to make eco-friendlier choices in their own lives.

Advocating for Environmental Policies in the Digital Nomad World

As digital nomads, you can play a crucial role in advocating for environmental policies and encouraging sustainable practices within the remote work and travel sectors. By using your influence and connections, you can help promote change and create an eco-friendlier digital nomad community. Here are some ways to advocate for environmental policies in the digital nomad world:

1. Engage with local authorities and organizations: During your travels, engage with local authorities, tourism boards, and environmental organizations to discuss the importance of sustainability and eco-friendly practices. Share your experiences and insights as a green digital nomad to help them understand the benefits of implementing environmental policies and initiatives.

2. Support eco-friendly businesses: Choose to work with and support businesses that prioritize sustainability and implement eco-friendly practices, such as green accommodations, coworking spaces, and tour operators. By supporting these businesses, you send a message that there is a demand for sustainable options within the digital nomad community.

3. Raise awareness through your platforms: Use your blog, social media, podcasts, or other platforms to raise awareness about environmental issues and the importance of implementing eco-friendly policies. Share information about successful initiatives, campaigns, and policies from around the world to inspire change in the digital nomad community.

4. Collaborate with other eco-conscious digital nomads: Join forces with other green digital nomads to create a unified voice advocating for environmental policies. Collaborate on projects, campaigns, or initiatives that promote sustainability within the remote work and travel sectors.

5. Participate in or organize events: Attend or organize events, conferences, webinars, or workshops focused on sustainability and environmental policies in the digital nomad world. Use

these platforms to discuss the importance of eco-friendly practices, share your experiences, and advocate for policy changes.

6. Lobby for policy changes: Contact policymakers, government officials, and industry leaders to advocate for the implementation of environmental policies that support sustainable practices within the digital nomad community. Share your insights, experiences, and suggestions on how these policies can benefit both the environment and the remote work industry.

7. Encourage corporate responsibility: As a digital nomad, you may work with various clients or companies. Encourage these organizations to adopt environmentally responsible practices and policies, such as reducing their carbon footprint, minimizing waste, or supporting eco-friendly initiatives.

By advocating for environmental policies in the digital nomad world, you can help create a more sustainable future for both the remote work industry and the planet. Your efforts can inspire change, promote eco-friendly practices, and contribute to a greener, more responsible digital nomad community.

CONCLUSION

Embracing Sustainable Living as a Digital Nomad

As a digital nomad, you have a unique opportunity to make a positive impact on the environment by embracing sustainable living and eco-friendly practices. Adopting a green lifestyle not only benefits the planet but also enriches your own experiences, relationships, and personal growth.

Incorporating sustainable practices into your travel, work, and daily living routines can help you reduce your environmental footprint and contribute to a more sustainable future. By choosing eco-friendly transportation, supporting green accommodations, adopting energy-efficient work habits, and making conscious choices in your daily life, you can significantly minimize your carbon emissions and overall environmental impact.

Building a network of like-minded, eco-conscious digital nomads can provide valuable support and inspiration as you navigate the challenges and rewards of sustainable living. Sharing your journey with others and advocating for environmental policies can help create a more responsible and environmentally aware digital nomad community.

As you continue to explore the world and work remotely, remember that every small action and choice contributes to a larger movement towards sustainability. Embrace the opportunity to create a positive impact on the environment, and inspire others to do the same, as you enjoy the freedom and adventure that comes with being a green digital nomad.

The Ongoing Journey to a Greener Lifestyle

Embarking on a greener lifestyle is a continuous journey of learning, adapting, and making conscious choices to minimize your environmental impact. As a digital nomad, you have the unique opportunity to influence and inspire others as you travel and work around the world. Embracing sustainability in your life is an ongoing process, and here are some ways to keep growing and evolving on this path:

1. Stay informed: Keep up-to-date with the latest news, research, and developments in sustainability, eco-friendly practices, and environmental policies. Staying informed will help you make better choices and adapt to new technologies or strategies that can enhance your green lifestyle.

2. Learn from others: Connect with other eco-conscious digital nomads, travellers, and locals to exchange ideas, tips, and experiences. Learning from others can provide fresh perspectives and insights, helping you to continue improving your sustainable practices.

3. Reflect on your choices: Regularly assess your lifestyle choices and their environmental impact. Reflect on the changes you have made and identify areas where you can continue to grow and make eco-friendlier choices.

4. Be adaptable: As you continue your green journey, be open to new ideas, approaches, and technologies. Be prepared to adapt and modify your practices as you discover more effective and sustainable ways of living.

5. Share your experiences: Document and share your greener lifestyle journey with others through blogging, social media, podcasts, or other platforms. Your story can inspire and motivate others to adopt more sustainable practices in their own lives.

6. Set achievable goals: Establish short-term and long-term goals for your greener lifestyle journey. These goals can help you stay focused, motivated, and committed to making continuous improvements in your sustainable practices.

7. Celebrate your successes: Acknowledge and celebrate your achievements and progress on your green journey. Recognize the positive impact your choices have on the environment and use these successes to fuel your ongoing commitment to sustainability.

8. Encourage others: Support and encourage others to embark on their own green journey. Share your knowledge, experiences, and resources to help them make more environmentally conscious choices.

Remember, the journey to a greener lifestyle is an ongoing process that requires commitment, reflection, and adaptation. By continually learning, growing, and sharing your experiences, you can make a lasting positive impact on the environment and inspire others to join you in creating a more sustainable world.

The Global Impact of Green Digital Nomadism

As digital nomadism becomes increasingly popular, the potential for a collective impact on the environment grows as well. Green digital nomadism, or the conscious effort to minimize one's ecological footprint while working and traveling, has the potential to significantly contribute to global sustainability efforts. Here are some ways in which green digital nomadism can have a positive global impact:

1. Reduced carbon emissions: By choosing eco-friendly transportation, adopting slow travel practices, and offsetting carbon emissions, green digital nomads can help reduce their overall carbon footprint. This collective effort can contribute to the global fight against climate change.

2. Promoting sustainable tourism: Green digital nomads can support sustainable tourism by choosing environmentally responsible accommodations, participating in eco-friendly activities, and engaging with local communities in a respectful and sustainable manner. This can lead to a more responsible tourism industry that prioritizes environmental conservation and community well-being.

3. Raising awareness: By sharing their experiences and advocating for environmental policies, green digital nomads can raise awareness about the importance of sustainable living and travel. This increased awareness can inspire others to adopt eco-friendly practices and create a ripple effect of positive change.

4. Supporting local economies: Green digital nomads often prioritize supporting local businesses, artisans, and initiatives that promote sustainability and social responsibility. This can lead to economic growth that benefits local communities while also promoting environmental conservation.

5. Encouraging corporate responsibility: As remote workers, green digital nomads can influence their clients or employers to adopt environmentally friendly practices and policies. This can lead to more sustainable business models and contribute to a global shift towards corporate responsibility.

6. Creating a global network: By connecting with other eco-conscious digital nomads, green digital nomads can create a global network of individuals who share resources, knowledge, and experiences. This collective effort can lead to the development of innovative solutions and strategies for promoting sustainability on a global scale.

7. Inspiring cultural exchange: Green digital nomads often engage in cultural exchanges with the communities they visit, sharing their values of environmental responsibility and learning from local sustainable practices. This exchange of ideas can help foster a more inclusive and diverse global perspective on sustainability.

By adopting sustainable practices, green digital nomads can have a meaningful and lasting impact on the environment, local communities, and the global effort towards sustainability. As more digital nomads embrace eco-friendly practices, the collective impact of their actions can contribute to a more responsible and sustainable world for all.

APPENDICES

Resources for Green Digital Nomads

There are numerous resources available for green digital nomads to help them make eco-friendlier choices in their work, travel, and daily lives. These resources can provide valuable information, support, and inspiration for those looking to reduce their environmental impact. Here is a list of resources that can be useful for green digital nomads:

1. **Websites and blogs:**
   - Sustainable Travel International (https://sustainabletravel.org/)
   - Green Global Travel (https://greenglobaltravel.com/)
   - The Sustainable Nomad (https://thesustainablenomad.com/)
   - EcoCult (https://ecocult.com/)

2. **Mobile apps:**
   - HappyCow (find vegan and vegetarian restaurants)
   - Zero Waste App (locate zero waste shops, farmers markets, and bulk stores)
   - Ecosia (a search engine that plants trees with its ad revenue)
   - JouleBug (track and improve your sustainable habits)

3. **Books:**
   - "The Green Travel Guide" by Greg Neale
   - "Sustainable Travel: The Essential Guide to Positive Impact Adventures" by Holly Tuppen
   - "The Art of Slow Travel" by Dan Kieran
   - "Digital Minimalism" by Cal Newport

4. **Podcasts:**
   - The Sustainable Jungle Podcast
   - The Slow Travel Podcast
   - The Thoughtful Travel Podcast
   - Green Dreamer Podcast

5. **Online courses and webinars:**
   - Sustainable Travel International (webinars on sustainable travel and tourism)
   - Coursera (online courses on sustainability, climate change, and environmental science)
   - FutureLearn (free online courses on sustainable living, eco-friendly practices, and more)

6. **Social media communities and forums:**
   - Green Digital Nomad Facebook groups
   - Subreddits like r/ZeroWaste, r/Sustainable, r/DigitalNomad, and r/OneBag
   - Online forums dedicated to sustainable living and eco-friendly travel

7. **Carbon offset programs:**
   - Gold Standard (https://www.goldstandard.org/)
   - Cool Effect (https://www.cooleffect.org/)
   - ClimateCare (https://climatecare.org/)
   - Atmosfair (https://www.atmosfair.de/en/)

8. **Green accommodation directories:**
   - Green Key (https://www.greenkey.global/)
   - Green Pearls (https://www.greenpearls.com/)
   - Ecobnb (https://ecobnb.com/)
   - BookDifferent (https://www.bookdifferent.com/)

By utilizing these resources, green digital nomads can access valuable information, tips, and support to help them make more environmentally responsible choices in their work, travel, and daily lives. These resources can serve as a foundation for continuous learning and improvement, enabling digital nomads to reduce their environmental impact and contribute to a more sustainable future.

Glossary of Eco-Friendly Terms

Here is a glossary of some common eco-friendly terms to help you better understand the language of sustainability and green living:

1. Biodiversity: The variety and variability of life on Earth, including the number of different species, the genetic diversity within species, and the variety of ecosystems.
2. Carbon footprint: The total amount of greenhouse gas emissions (mainly carbon dioxide) that result from human activities, such as transportation, energy production, and consumption.

3. Climate change: A long-term change in the Earth's climate, primarily due to human activities, such as the burning of fossil fuels, deforestation, and other industrial processes that release large amounts of greenhouse gases into the atmosphere.

4. Carbon offsetting: The process of compensating for one's carbon emissions by supporting projects or initiatives that reduce greenhouse gas emissions elsewhere.

5. Circular economy: An economic system that aims to eliminate waste and pollution, keep products and materials in use, and regenerate natural systems.

6. Conservation: The protection, preservation, management, or restoration of natural environments, ecosystems, and wildlife.

7. Eco-friendly: Products or practices that have a minimal negative impact on the environment.

8. Ecosystem: A community of living organisms (plants, animals, and microbes) interacting with their physical environment and each other.

9. Energy efficiency: The ability to produce or use energy in a way that minimizes waste and maximizes the output or usefulness of the energy consumed.

10. Greenhouse gases (GHGs): Gases that trap heat in the Earth's atmosphere, leading to the greenhouse effect and global warming. The main greenhouse gases include carbon dioxide, methane, and nitrous oxide.

11. Renewable energy: Energy derived from natural resources that can be replenished over time, such as sunlight, wind, rain, and geothermal heat.

12. Slow travel: A mindful approach to travel that emphasizes longer stays, deeper connections with local communities, and reduced environmental impact.

13. Sustainable development: Development that meets the needs of the present without compromising the ability of future generations to meet their own needs.

14. Sustainable tourism: Tourism that seeks to minimize its negative impact on the environment, local culture, and economy while providing a positive experience for both visitors and host communities.

15. Zero waste: A philosophy that encourages the redesign of resource life cycles to minimize waste and keep materials in use, ultimately aiming for no trash sent to landfills or incinerators.

These terms are commonly used when discussing eco-friendly practices, environmental issues, and sustainability. Familiarizing yourself with this vocabulary can help you better understand the conversations surrounding green living and the environment.

Further Reading on Sustainable Living and Travel

If you're interested in learning more about sustainable living and travel, there are many books, websites, and resources available to explore. Here are some recommendations for further reading:

Books:
1. "Sustainable Travel: The Essential Guide to Positive Impact Adventures" by Holly Tuppen
2. "The Green Travel Guide" by Greg Neale
3. "The Art of Slow Travel" by Dan Kieran
4. "The Responsible Traveler's Guide to Southeast Asia" by Dr. Linda Chia
5. "Overbooked: The Exploding Business of Travel and Tourism" by Elizabeth Becker
6. "The Zero Waste Home" by Bea Johnson

7. "Plastic Free: How I Kicked the Plastic Habit and How You Can Too" by Beth Terry
8. "The Story of Stuff: How Our Obsession with Stuff Is Trashing the Planet, Our Communities, and Our Health—and a Vision for Change" by Annie Leonard
9. "Cradle to Cradle: Remaking the Way We Make Things" by William McDonough and Michael Braungart
10. "The Upcycle: Beyond Sustainability – Designing for Abundance" by William McDonough and Michael Braungart

Websites and blogs:
1. Sustainable Travel International (https://sustainabletravel.org/)
2. Green Global Travel (https://greenglobaltravel.com/)
3. The Sustainable Nomad (https://thesustainablenomad.com/)
4. Ecocult (https://ecocult.com/)
5. The Good Trade (https://www.thegoodtrade.com/)
6. Going Zero Waste (https://www.goingzerowaste.com/)
7. Green Matters (https://www.greenmatters.com/)

Podcasts:
1. The Sustainable Jungle Podcast
2. The Slow Travel Podcast
3. The Thoughtful Travel Podcast
4. Green Dreamer Podcast

These resources cover various aspects of sustainable living and travel, from practical advice on reducing waste and conserving resources to exploring the broader social, economic, and environmental impacts of tourism. By delving into these books, websites, and podcasts, you can expand your knowledge and understanding of sustainable living and travel and discover new ways to incorporate eco-friendly practices into your daily life.

www.ingramcontent.com/pod-product-compliance
Lightning Source LLC
Chambersburg PA
CBHW070913220526
45466CB00005B/2203